Caption

DYNAMIC SALES MASTERY

Empowering Sales Professionals

By Sanjay Nakrani

This book is devoted to all the sales people worldwide, whose commitment, enthusiasm, and fortitude drive the wheels of business.

I hope these pages provide you with the knowledge, understanding, and motivation you need to lead a dynamic sales mastery path. The success of our firm is largely due to your dedication and hard work. You are the unsung heroes of the sales industry, and we salute you.

INTRODUCTION

Welcome to "Dynamic Sales Mastery: Empowering Sales Professionals," a comprehensive guide designed to equip you with the knowledge, skills, and strategies to excel in the dynamic world of sales. In this book, we will explore the key principles, techniques, and best practices that define successful sales professionals and empower you to achieve your full potential in the field of sales.

In today's fast-paced and competitive marketplace, mastering the art of sales is more important than ever. This book is for everyone in the sales industry, whether you are an experienced sales professional wishing to improve your abilities or a novice trying to make a name for yourself as a top performer. We will explore the psychology of selling, successful communication strategies, relationship- and rapport-building, overcoming objections, strategic prospecting, negotiating approaches, time management, technology utilisation, maintaining success, and a host of other topics.

Throughout these pages, you'll find practical insights, actionable strategies, real-world examples, and exercises to help you apply what you learn to your own sales efforts. By mastering the principles of dynamic sales, you'll be able to connect with customers on a deeper level, anticipate their needs, and provide value that sets you apart from the competition. Whether you're selling products, services, or ideas, the principles of dynamic sales mastery are universal and can be applied across industries and contexts.

So, if you're ready to take your sales career to the next level, dive into "Dynamic Sales Mastery: Empowering Sales Professionals" and embark on a journey of growth, learning, and success.

Together, we'll unlock the secrets to becoming a truly dynamic sales professional.

CONTENTS:

Chapter 1: The Selling Psychology

1.1 Understanding Buyer Behaviour
1.2 Building Emotional Connections
1.3 Influencing Purchase Decisions

Chapter 2: Effective Communication Techniques

2.1 Active Listening Skills
2.2 The Power of Persuasive Language
2.3 Nonverbal Communication Strategies
2.4 Emotional Intelligence in Communication
2.5 Adaptability in Communication

Chapter 3: Building Rapport and Relationships

3.1 Establishing Trust and Credibility
3.2 Nurturing Long-Term Partnerships
3.3 Personalising the Sales Experience
3.4 Active Listening and Empathy
3.5 Consistent Communication and Follow-Up

Chapter 4: Overcoming Objections and Rejections

4.1 Understanding the Nature of Objections
4.2 Handling Objections with Empathy and Understanding
4.3 Turning Rejections into Opportunities
4.4 Preemptive Objection Handling
4.5 Closing the Sale After Overcoming Objections

Chapter 5: Strategic Prospecting and Lead Generation

5.1 Identifying Ideal Prospects
5.2 Developing Targeted Outreach Strategies
5.3 Qualifying Leads Effectively
5.4 Leveraging Technology for Lead Generation
5.5 Nurturing Leads and Building Relationships

Chapter 6: The Art of Negotiation

6.1 Understanding the Principles of Negotiation
6.2 Preparation and Planning
6.3 Communication and Persuasion Skills
6.4 Flexibility and Adaptability
6.5 Closing the Deal and Building Relationships

Chapter 7: Time Management and Productivity

7.1 Importance of Effective Time Management
7.2 Prioritising Tasks and Setting Goals
7.3 Eliminating Time Wasters and Distractions
7.4 Utilising Time Management Tools and Techniques
7.5 Continuous Improvement and Learning

Chapter 8: Leveraging Technology for Sales Success

8.1 The Role of Technology in Modern Sales
8.2 CRM Systems for Customer Relationship Management
8.3 Sales Automation and AI-Powered Tools
8.4 Social Selling and Digital Engagement Platforms
8.5 Continuous Learning and Adaptation to New Technologies

Chapter 9: Sustaining Success and Growth

9.1 The Importance of Consistent Performance
9.2 Building and Nurturing Relationships
9.3 Continuous Learning and Professional Development

9.4 Innovation and Adaptation to Market Trends
9.5 Strategic Planning and Goal Setting

Chapter 10: Mastering Sales Leadership

10.1 The Role of Sales Leadership in Success
10.2 Leading by Example
10.3 Communication and Collaboration
10.4 Developing and Mentoring Sales Talent
10.5 Strategic Vision and Decision-Making

Chapter 11: Building a Personal Brand

11.1 Understanding Personal Branding
11.2 Crafting Your Brand Message
11.3 Visibility and Presence
11.4 Leveraging Social Media
11.5 Networking and Relationships
11.6 Continual Learning and Adaptation

Chapter 12: Achieving Work-Life Balance

12.1 Understanding Work-Life Balance
12.2 Setting Boundaries
12.3 Time Management Skills
12.4 The Role of Technology
12.5 Building Support Systems
12.6 Regular Self-Assessment

THE SELLING PSYCHOLOGY

1.1 Understanding Buyer Behaviour

In the world of sales, understanding buyer behaviour is paramount. A complex interaction of emotions, motivations, and cognitive processes affects every purchase choice. Understanding the psychology of your clients will help you modify your strategy so that it speaks to their wants and requirements.

Buyers are not just making rational decisions based on product features or price; they are also influenced by emotional factors, social proof, and their own self-perception. For instance, a customer may choose a product because it makes them feel successful, secure, or valued. Understanding these underlying motivations can help you craft a more compelling sales pitch and connect with your customers on a deeper level.

Key Benefits:

- **Enhanced Understanding:** Gain a deeper insight into what drives your customers' purchasing decisions.
- **Tailored Approach:** Customise your sales strategy to resonate with your customers' needs and desires.
- **Increased Sales Effectiveness:** Connect with customers on an emotional level, leading to higher conversion rates and customer satisfaction.

1.2 Building Emotional Connections

Emotions play a significant role in the buying process. Customers are more likely to make a purchase when they feel a strong emotional connection to a product, brand, or salesperson. As a sales professional, your ability to empathise with your customers' emotions and build genuine relationships can set you apart from the competition.

Building emotional connections involves active listening, empathy, and authenticity. By truly understanding your customers' needs and concerns, you can address them effectively and position your product or service as the solution they've been searching for. This not only boosts sales but also fosters long-term loyalty and customer advocacy.

Key Benefits:

- **Increased Customer Loyalty:** Build trust and rapport with your customers, leading to repeat business and referrals.
- **Higher Conversion Rates:** Emotional connections can lead to quicker decision-making and higher conversion rates.
- **Stronger Brand Advocacy:** Satisfied customers are more likely to recommend your products or services to others, amplifying your brand's reach.

1.3 Influencing Purchase Decisions

As a sales professional, your ultimate goal is to influence purchase decisions in your favour. Understanding the psychological triggers that influence buying behaviour can give you a competitive edge and empower you to guide customers towards choosing your product or service.

There are various psychological principles at play when it comes to influencing purchase decisions, such as scarcity, social proof, and authority. By incorporating these principles into your sales strategy, you can create a sense of urgency, build credibility, and persuade customers to take action.

Key Benefits:

- **Effective Persuasion:** Develop your persuasive skills by using psychological concepts to change people's decisions to buy.
- **Competitive Advantage:** Stand out from the competition by understanding and addressing the psychological needs of your customers.
- **Increased Sales Revenue:** By influencing purchase decisions effectively, you can drive sales and revenue growth for your business.

Understanding the psychology of selling is not just about manipulating customers into buying; it's about creating win-win situations where both parties benefit. By aligning your sales approach with the psychological needs and motivations of your customers, you can create a more fulfilling and successful sales experience for everyone involved.

In the following chapters, we will go through deeper into specific psychological principles and techniques that you can apply to enhance your sales effectiveness and achieve dynamic sales mastery.

EFFECTIVE COMMUNICATION TECHNIQUES

2.1 Active Listening Skills

Active listening is a cornerstone of effective communication. It involves fully concentrating, understanding, responding, and remembering what the other person is saying. By practicing active listening in your sales interactions, you demonstrate respect and empathy towards your customers, making them feel valued and understood.

Benefits:

- **Enhanced Understanding:** Gain deeper insight into customer needs and concerns.
- **Building Trust:** Show customers that their opinions and feelings are important.
- **Effective Problem-Solving:** Identify and address customer issues more effectively.

2.2 The Power of Persuasive Language

The words you choose can have a significant impact on how your message is received. Using persuasive language that resonates with your customers' emotions, values, and desires can make your sales pitch more compelling and convincing. By mastering the art of persuasive language, you can influence customer perceptions and drive them towards making a purchase.

Benefits:

- **Increased Engagement:** Capture and maintain customer attention.
- **Effective Influence:** Persuade customers to see the value in your product or service.
- **Higher Conversion Rates:** Convert leads into customers more effectively.

2.3 Nonverbal Communication Strategies

Nonverbal communication, such as body language, facial expressions, and tone of voice, plays a crucial role in conveying your message effectively. Being aware of and managing your nonverbal cues can enhance your communication skills and help you build rapport with customers. By aligning your verbal and nonverbal communication, you can create a cohesive and impactful sales presentation.

Benefits:

- **Building Rapport:** Establish a strong connection with customers through nonverbal cues.
- **Enhanced Clarity:** Reinforce your verbal message with consistent nonverbal signals.
- **Improved Relationships:** Strengthen relationships with customers through effective nonverbal communication.

2.4 Emotional Intelligence in Communication

Emotional intelligence (EI) extends beyond understanding and managing your own emotions; it also involves recognising and responding to the emotions of others. By applying EI principles in your communication, you can build stronger relationships with customers, handle objections with empathy, and navigate challenging situations with grace.

Benefits:

- **Stronger Relationships:** Foster trust and rapport through emotionally intelligent communication.
- **Effective Conflict Resolution:** Handle objections and disagreements with empathy and understanding.
- **Customer Satisfaction:** Enhance customer satisfaction by addressing emotional needs and concerns.

2.5 Adaptability in Communication

Every customer is unique, and adapting your communication style to meet their needs and preferences is essential for effective communication. Whether it's adjusting your tone, pacing, or content, being adaptable in your communication allows you to connect with a diverse range of customers and build stronger relationships.

Benefits:

- **Improved Connection:** Connect with customers on a personal level by adapting your communication style.
- **Customer-Centric Approach:** Tailor your communication to meet customer needs and preferences.
- **Enhanced Sales Effectiveness:** Increase your chances of success by communicating in a way that resonates with customers.

Effective communication is a critical skill for sales professionals. By mastering active listening, persuasive language, nonverbal communication, emotional intelligence, and adaptability, you can enhance your communication skills and become a more effective and influential salesperson.

In the following chapters, we'll delve deeper into each of these communication techniques, providing you with practical tips, strategies, and exercises to help you apply them in your sales interactions and achieve dynamic sales mastery.

BUILDING RAPPORT AND RELATIONSHIPS

3.1 Establishing Trust and Credibility

Building trust and credibility is the foundation of any successful sales relationship. Customers are more likely to do business with people they trust and believe in. By demonstrating honesty, reliability, and integrity in your interactions, you can establish yourself as a trustworthy and credible sales professional.

Benefits:

- **Long-Term Relationships:** Foster lasting relationships based on trust and credibility.
- **Repeat Business:** Encourage repeat business and customer loyalty.
- **Referrals:** Gain referrals from satisfied customers who trust your expertise.

3.2 Nurturing Long-Term Partnerships

Aim to build long-term partnerships with your customers rather than focusing solely on making a sale. By investing time and effort in understanding their needs, preferences, and challenges, you can offer personalised solutions that add value and demonstrate your commitment to their success.

Benefits:

- **Customer Loyalty:** Cultivate customer loyalty through personalised, long-term partnerships.
- **Value-Added Solutions:** Provide solutions that address specific customer needs and challenges.
- **Stable Revenue:** Achieve stable revenue streams through repeat business and long-term contracts.

3.3 Personalising the Sales Experience

Personalisation is key to creating memorable and impactful sales experiences. By taking the time to understand your customers' unique needs, preferences, and aspirations, you can tailor your sales approach to resonate with them on a deeper level. This personalised approach not only enhances customer satisfaction but also increases your chances of closing the sale.

Benefits:

- **Enhanced Engagement:** Capture and maintain customer attention with personalised sales experiences.
- **Higher Conversion Rates:** Increase conversion rates by aligning your offerings with customer needs.
- **Customer Satisfaction:** Improve customer satisfaction by delivering personalised solutions and experiences.

3.4 Active Listening and Empathy

Active listening and empathy are essential skills for building rapport and relationships. By truly listening to your customers' concerns, feelings, and aspirations, and demonstrating empathy in your responses, you can build a stronger connection and foster trust and understanding.

Benefits:

- **Stronger Connections:** Build stronger, more meaningful connections with customers.
- **Trust and Understanding:** Foster trust and understanding through active listening and empathy.
- **Effective Problem-Solving:** Identify and address customer issues more effectively by truly understanding their perspective.

3.5 Consistent Communication and Follow-Up

Consistency in communication and follow-up is crucial for maintaining and strengthening relationships with customers. Regularly checking in, providing updates, and seeking feedback shows customers that you value their business and are committed to their success.

Benefits:

- **Relationship Maintenance:** Maintain strong relationships through consistent communication and follow-up.
- **Customer Satisfaction:** Improve customer satisfaction by keeping them informed and engaged.
- **Opportunity Identification:** Identify new opportunities for upselling or cross-selling through regular interactions.

Building rapport and relationships is an ongoing process that requires time, effort, and genuine commitment. By focusing on establishing trust and credibility, nurturing long-term partnerships, personalising the sales experience, practicing active listening and empathy, and maintaining consistent communication and follow-up, you can build strong and enduring relationships with your customers.

In the following chapters, we'll explore specific strategies and techniques to help you further enhance your relationship-building skills and achieve dynamic sales mastery.

OVERCOMING OBJECTIONS AND REJECTIONS

4.1 Understanding the Nature of Objections

Objections are a natural part of the sales process and often indicate that the customer has questions, concerns, or reservations about your product or service. By viewing objections as opportunities for clarification rather than roadblocks, you can address them effectively and move closer to closing the sale.

Benefits:

- **Clarification:** Gain insight into customer concerns and questions.
- **Increased Confidence:** Approach objections with confidence and professionalism.
- **Progression in Sales Process:** Use objections as stepping stones towards closing the sale.

4.2 Handling Objections with Empathy and Understanding

Empathy and understanding are key when addressing objections. By acknowledging and validating your customers' concerns, you demonstrate that you value their perspective and are committed to finding a solution that meets their needs.

Benefits:

- **Building Trust:** Foster trust by showing empathy and understanding.
- **Effective Communication:** Improve communication by addressing objections directly.
- **Customer Satisfaction:** Increase customer satisfaction by resolving concerns effectively.

4.3 Turning Rejections into Opportunities

Not every sale will result in a closed deal, and that's okay. Rejections can be valuable learning experiences that provide insights into areas for improvement or opportunities for future engagement. By adopting a positive mindset and viewing rejections as opportunities for growth, you can learn from each experience and become a more resilient and successful salesperson.

Benefits:

- **Continuous Learning:** Learn from rejections to improve your sales approach.
- **Resilience:** Develop resilience by overcoming rejections and setbacks.
- **Future Opportunities:** Identify opportunities for future engagement or follow-up.

4.4 Preemptive Objection Handling

Anticipating and addressing potential objections proactively can help you maintain control of the sales conversation and steer it towards a positive outcome. By preparing responses to common objections in advance, you can demonstrate your expertise, build credibility, and reassure customers that you understand their concerns.

Benefits:

- **Professionalism:** Demonstrate professionalism by anticipating and addressing objections proactively.
- **Credibility:** Build credibility by providing well-thought-out responses to objections.
- **Control of Conversation:** Maintain control of the sales conversation by steering it towards a positive outcome.

4.5 Closing the Sale After Overcoming Objections

Successfully overcoming objections is often the final hurdle in closing the sale. By addressing objections effectively, building trust, and demonstrating the value of your product or service, you can create a compelling case that motivates customers to take action and make a purchase.

Benefits:

- **Increased Sales Success:** Improve your chances of closing the sale by overcoming objections.
- **Customer Satisfaction:** Ensure that customers feel confident in their purchase decision.
- **Achieving Sales Goals:** Reach and exceed your sales targets by closing more deals.

Overcoming objections and rejections is a critical skill for sales professionals. By understanding the nature of objections, handling them with empathy and understanding, turning rejections into opportunities, engaging in preemptive objection handling, and successfully closing the sale, you can enhance your sales effectiveness and achieve dynamic sales mastery.

In the following chapters, we'll delve deeper into specific strategies and techniques to help you further refine your objection-handling skills and achieve greater success in your sales career.

STRATEGIC PROSPECTING AND LEAD GENERATION

5.1 Identifying Ideal Prospects

Effective prospecting begins with identifying and targeting the right prospects for your product or service. By understanding your target market, customer personas, and ideal customer profiles, you can focus your efforts on prospects who are most likely to be interested in what you have to offer.

Benefits:

- **Efficiency:** Focus your efforts on prospects who are a good fit for your offering.
- **Higher Conversion Rates:** Increase your chances of converting leads into customers.
- **Improved ROI:** Maximise return on investment by targeting the right prospects.

5.2 Developing Targeted Outreach Strategies

Once you've identified your ideal prospects, the next step is to develop targeted outreach strategies to engage them effectively. Whether it's through email marketing, social media, networking events, or cold calling, tailoring your approach to the preferences and behaviours of your target audience can enhance your prospecting efforts.

Benefits:

- **Personalisation:** Engage prospects with tailored messaging and offers.
- **Increased Engagement:** Boost prospect engagement with relevant and timely outreach.
- **Brand Awareness:** Raise awareness of your brand among your target audience.

5.3 Qualifying Leads Effectively

Qualifying leads effectively is essential for focusing your time and resources on prospects who are most likely to convert into customers. By establishing criteria for lead qualification based on factors such as interest level, budget, authority, and need, you can prioritise your efforts and pursue opportunities that align with your sales objectives.

Benefits:

- **Focused Efforts:** Prioritise prospects that align with your sales objectives.
- **Improved Sales Efficiency:** Allocate resources more efficiently by focusing on qualified leads.
- **Higher Quality Opportunities:** Pursue opportunities with a higher likelihood of conversion.

5.4 Leveraging Technology for Lead Generation

Technology plays a crucial role in modern lead generation strategies. Utilising CRM systems, marketing automation tools, and data analytics can streamline your lead generation process, enhance your targeting capabilities, and provide valuable insights to optimise your prospecting efforts.

Benefits:

- **Streamlined Process:** Automate manual tasks to streamline your lead generation process.
- **Enhanced Targeting:** Utilise data analytics to refine your targeting and segmentation strategies.
- **Data-Driven Decisions:** Make informed decisions based on data and analytics to optimise your lead generation efforts.

5.5 Nurturing Leads and Building Relationships

Lead generation is not just about acquiring new leads; it's also about nurturing them and building long-term relationships. By providing valuable content, staying in regular contact, and demonstrating your expertise and value over time, you can build trust and credibility with your leads, increasing the likelihood of conversion.

Benefits:

- **Building Trust:** Foster trust and credibility with leads through ongoing engagement and relationship-building.
- **Long-Term Success:** Increase the lifetime value of customers by nurturing leads effectively.
- **Customer Retention:** Improve customer retention rates by maintaining strong relationships post-sale.

Strategic prospecting and lead generation are foundational elements of a successful sales strategy. By identifying ideal prospects, developing targeted outreach strategies, qualifying leads effectively, leveraging technology, and nurturing leads and building relationships, you can enhance your prospecting efforts and achieve dynamic sales mastery.

In the following chapters, we'll explore specific tactics and techniques to help you further refine your prospecting and lead generation skills and achieve greater success in your sales career.

THE ART OF NEGOTIATION

6.1 Understanding the Principles of Negotiation

Negotiation is a fundamental skill in sales that involves reaching mutually beneficial agreements through dialogue and compromise. Understanding the principles of negotiation, such as preparation, communication, flexibility, and problem-solving, is essential for achieving successful outcomes and building long-term relationships with customers.

Benefits:

- **Win-Win Outcomes:** Achieve agreements that benefit both parties.
- **Relationship Building:** Strengthen relationships with customers through effective negotiation.
- **Value Maximisation:** Maximise the value of deals by negotiating effectively.

6.2 Preparation and Planning

Preparation is key to successful negotiation. Researching the customer, understanding their needs and priorities, and identifying potential concessions and trade-offs in advance can give you a competitive advantage and increase your confidence during negotiations.

Benefits:

- **Confidence:** Approach negotiations with confidence and preparedness.
- **Control:** Maintain control of the negotiation process by being well-prepared.
- **Better Outcomes:** Increase the likelihood of achieving favourable outcomes through thorough preparation.

6.3 Communication and Persuasion Skills

Effective communication and persuasion skills are essential for conveying your value proposition, addressing concerns, and influencing decision-making during negotiations. By mastering the art of persuasive communication, you can build rapport with customers, overcome objections, and guide discussions towards mutually beneficial agreements.

Benefits:

- **Building Rapport:** Establish trust and rapport with customers through effective communication.
- **Overcoming Objections:** Address and overcome objections with persuasive arguments.
- **Influencing Decisions:** Influence customer decisions in your favour through compelling communication.

6.4 Flexibility and Adaptability

Flexibility and adaptability are crucial during negotiations, as they allow you to respond to changing circumstances, unexpected challenges, and differing viewpoints effectively. By remaining open-minded and flexible, you can explore alternative solutions, find common ground, and adapt your approach to achieve the best possible outcome.

Benefits:

- **Adaptability:** Adapt your negotiation strategy to respond to changing circumstances.
- **Finding Common Ground:** Explore alternative solutions and find common ground with customers.
- **Resolving Challenges:** Overcome unexpected challenges and objections with flexibility and creativity.

6.5 Closing the Deal and Building Relationships

Closing the deal is the culmination of effective negotiation skills. By reaching an agreement that satisfies both parties and finalising the details in a clear and transparent manner, you can build trust and credibility with customers, setting the stage for long-term relationships and future opportunities.

Benefits:

- **Trust and Credibility:** Build trust and credibility by finalising agreements in a transparent manner.
- **Long-Term Relationships:** Lay the foundation for long-term relationships and future opportunities.
- **Customer Satisfaction:** Ensure customer satisfaction by meeting their needs and expectations.

The art of negotiation is a complex and nuanced skill that requires preparation, communication, flexibility, and adaptability. By understanding the principles of negotiation, preparing thoroughly, mastering communication and persuasion skills, remaining flexible and adaptable, and closing deals effectively, you can enhance your negotiation capabilities and achieve dynamic sales mastery.

In the following chapters, we'll go through deeper into specific negotiation techniques, strategies, and scenarios to help you further refine your negotiation skills and achieve greater success in your sales career.

TIME MANAGEMENT AND PRODUCTIVITY

7.1 Importance of Effective Time Management

Effective time management is crucial for sales professionals to maximise productivity, meet deadlines, and achieve sales targets. By prioritising tasks, minimising distractions, and allocating time wisely, you can make the most of your working hours and maintain a healthy work-life balance.

Benefits:

- **Increased Productivity:** Accomplish more in less time by prioritising tasks effectively.
- **Meeting Deadlines:** Ensure timely completion of projects and tasks.
- **Work-Life Balance:** Maintain a healthy balance between work and personal life.

7.2 Prioritising Tasks and Setting Goals

Prioritising tasks and setting clear, achievable goals are essential for staying focused and organised. By identifying high-priority tasks and aligning them with your sales objectives, you can stay on track and make progress towards your targets more efficiently.

Benefits:

- **Focus:** Maintain focus on high-priority tasks that align with your sales objectives.
- **Achieving Goals:** Make steady progress towards your sales targets by setting clear goals.
- **Motivation:** Stay motivated and accountable by tracking your progress and achievements.

7.3 Eliminating Time Wasters and Distractions

Identifying and eliminating time wasters and distractions can significantly boost your productivity. Whether it's unnecessary meetings, excessive multitasking, or social media scrolling, reducing distractions allows you to concentrate on tasks that contribute to your sales success.

Benefits:

- **Improved Focus:** Concentrate on important tasks without distractions.
- **Efficiency:** Complete tasks more efficiently by eliminating time wasters.
- **Quality of Work:** Improve the quality of your work by focusing on what truly matters.

7.4 Utilising Time Management Tools and Techniques

Utilising time management tools and techniques can help you organise your tasks, track your time, and optimise your workflow. Whether it's using a digital calendar, task management software, or the Pomodoro technique, finding the right tools and techniques can enhance your efficiency and effectiveness.

Benefits:

- **Organisation:** Keep track of tasks, deadlines, and appointments more effectively.

- **Optimised Workflow:** Streamline your workflow and eliminate bottlenecks.
- **Accountability:** Hold yourself accountable by tracking your time and progress.

7.5 Continuous Improvement and Learning

Continuous improvement and learning are key to staying ahead in today's competitive sales landscape. By regularly reviewing and refining your time management and productivity strategies, learning new skills, and adapting to changes, you can continuously improve your performance and achieve greater success in your sales career.

Benefits:

- **Adaptability:** Adapt to changes and challenges more effectively by learning continuously.
- **Skill Development:** Improve your time management and productivity skills through continuous learning.
- **Professional Growth:** Achieve greater success and career advancement by continuously improving your performance.

Time management and productivity are critical skills for sales professionals to master. By focusing on effective time management, prioritising tasks and setting goals, eliminating time wasters and distractions, utilising time management tools and techniques, and committing to continuous improvement and learning, you can enhance your productivity, achieve your sales targets, and achieve dynamic sales mastery.

In the following chapters, we'll explore specific time management tools, techniques, and strategies to help you further refine your time management and productivity skills and achieve greater success in your sales career.

LEVERAGING TECHNOLOGY FOR SALES SUCCESS

8.1 The Role of Technology in Modern Sales

Technology plays a pivotal role in modern sales by enabling sales professionals to streamline processes, enhance communication, and gain valuable insights into customer behaviour. Embracing technology can significantly boost sales efficiency, effectiveness, and success in today's digital age.

Benefits:

- **Streamlined Processes:** Automate repetitive tasks to save time and effort.
- **Enhanced Communication:** Improve communication with customers and team members.
- **Data-Driven Decisions:** Gain insights into customer behaviour and sales performance.

8.2 CRM Systems for Customer Relationship Management

CRM (Customer Relationship Management) systems are essential tools for managing customer interactions, tracking sales activities, and analysing customer data. By using a CRM system, sales professionals can build stronger relationships with customers, improve sales forecasting, and optimise their sales strategies.

Benefits:

- **Improved Customer Relationships:** Personalise interactions and build stronger relationships.
- **Sales Forecasting:** Predict sales trends and performance more accurately.
- **Optimised Sales Strategies:** Analyse data to refine and optimise sales strategies.

8.3 Sales Automation and AI-Powered Tools

Sales automation and AI-powered tools can automate repetitive tasks, personalise customer interactions, and provide predictive insights to sales professionals. By leveraging these tools, sales professionals can focus on high-value activities, enhance customer engagement, and make data-driven decisions.

Benefits:

- **Time Savings:** Automate repetitive tasks to focus on strategic activities.
- **Personalised Engagement:** Use AI to personalise customer interactions and offers.
- **Predictive Insights:** Utilise predictive analytics to forecast sales trends and opportunities.

8.4 Social Selling and Digital Engagement Platforms

Social selling and digital engagement platforms enable sales professionals to connect with customers, share content, and build relationships online. By leveraging these platforms, sales professionals can expand their reach, engage with customers on their preferred channels, and nurture leads effectively.

Benefits:

- **Expanded Reach:** Connect with a broader audience across various digital platforms.
- **Engagement:** Engage with customers in real-time through social selling.
- **Lead Nurturing:** Nurture leads effectively with targeted content and communication.

8.5 Continuous Learning and Adaptation to New Technologies

The world of technology is constantly evolving, with new tools, platforms, and technologies emerging regularly. Continuous learning and adaptation to new technologies are crucial for staying ahead in the competitive sales landscape and achieving long-term success.

Benefits:

- **Adaptability:** Stay ahead of the competition by adapting to new technologies.
- **Skill Development:** Improve your skills and knowledge through continuous learning.
- **Competitive Advantage:** Gain a competitive advantage by leveraging the latest technologies effectively.

Leveraging technology for sales success is essential in today's digital era. By embracing CRM systems for customer relationship management, utilising sales automation and AI-powered tools, engaging in social selling and digital platforms, and committing to continuous learning and adaptation, sales professionals can enhance their efficiency, effectiveness, and success in the competitive sales landscape.

In the following chapters, we'll explore specific technologies, tools, and strategies to help you further leverage technology for sales success and achieve dynamic sales mastery.

SUSTAINING SUCCESS AND GROWTH

9.1 The Importance of Consistent Performance

Consistency is key to sustaining success and growth in sales. Maintaining a high level of performance over time requires discipline, resilience, and a commitment to continuous improvement. By setting realistic goals, staying focused, and adapting to changing circumstances, you can sustain your success and achieve long-term growth.

Benefits:

- **Long-Term Success:** Maintain consistent performance to achieve long-term success.
- **Stability:** Create a stable foundation for sustainable growth.
- **Credibility:** Build credibility and trust with customers and stakeholders.

9.2 Building and Nurturing Relationships

Building and nurturing relationships with customers is essential for sustaining success and growth. By providing exceptional customer service, maintaining open communication, and going above and beyond to meet customer needs, you can foster loyalty, encourage repeat business, and generate referrals.

Benefits:

- **Customer Loyalty:** Foster loyalty and retain customers for long-term success.
- **Repeat Business:** Encourage repeat business through exceptional customer service.
- **Referrals:** Generate referrals by exceeding customer expectations and building strong relationships.

9.3 Continuous Learning and Professional Development

Continuous learning and professional development are crucial for staying ahead in the competitive sales landscape. By investing in your skills, knowledge, and personal growth, you can adapt to changes, seize new opportunities, and sustain your success over the long term.

Benefits:

- **Adaptability:** Adapt to changes and challenges more effectively through continuous learning.
- **Career Growth:** Enhance your career prospects and opportunities for advancement.
- **Competitive Advantage:** Gain a competitive advantage by staying ahead of industry trends and developments.

9.4 Innovation and Adaptation to Market Trends

Innovation and adaptation to market trends are essential for sustaining growth and staying competitive. By embracing new technologies, exploring new markets, and adapting your strategies to meet evolving customer needs, you can capitalise on opportunities and drive sustainable growth.

Benefits:

- **Market Leadership:** Establish market leadership by innovating and adapting to trends.
- **Business Growth:** Drive sustainable business growth by exploring new opportunities.
- **Customer Satisfaction:** Meet evolving customer needs and expectations through innovation.

9.5 Strategic Planning and Goal Setting

Strategic planning and goal setting are fundamental to sustaining success and achieving long-term growth. By setting clear, measurable goals, developing strategic plans, and regularly reviewing and adjusting your strategies, you can stay on track and ensure that your efforts are aligned with your objectives.

Benefits:

- **Alignment:** Align your efforts with your objectives through strategic planning.
- **Focus:** Maintain focus on key priorities and initiatives.
- **Accountability:** Hold yourself and your team accountable for achieving goals and targets.

Sustaining success and growth in sales requires a combination of consistent performance, relationship building, continuous learning, innovation, adaptation, strategic planning, and goal setting. By focusing on these key areas and committing to excellence in your sales efforts, you can achieve dynamic sales mastery and enjoy sustained success and growth in your sales career.

In the following chapters, we'll explore specific strategies, techniques, and best practices to help you sustain success and achieve long-term growth in your sales career.

MASTERING SALES LEADERSHIP

10.1 The Role of Sales Leadership in Success

Sales leadership plays a pivotal role in driving success, motivating teams, and achieving organisational goals. Effective sales leaders inspire, guide, and support their teams, fostering a culture of excellence, collaboration, and continuous improvement.

Benefits:

- **Team Motivation:** Inspire and motivate your team to achieve their best.
- **Culture of Excellence:** Foster a culture of excellence and continuous improvement.
- **Organisational Success:** Drive organisational success through effective leadership.

10.2 Leading by Example

Leading by example is a hallmark of effective sales leadership. By demonstrating professionalism, integrity, and a strong work ethic, sales leaders can set the standard for their teams and inspire them to emulate these qualities in their own work.

Benefits:

- **Trust and Respect:** Earn the trust and respect of your team by leading by example.
- **Inspiration:** Inspire your team to perform at their best by demonstrating excellence.
- **Positive Influence:** Positively influence team behaviour and performance through your actions.

10.3 Communication and Collaboration

Effective communication and collaboration are essential skills for sales leaders. By maintaining open lines of communication, encouraging collaboration, and fostering a supportive team environment, sales leaders can enhance team cohesion, productivity, and success.

Benefits:

- **Team Cohesion:** Build strong relationships and foster a cohesive team environment.
- **Productivity:** Boost team productivity through effective communication and collaboration.
- **Problem-Solving:** Encourage teamwork and collaboration to solve challenges more effectively.

10.4 Developing and Mentoring Sales Talent

Developing and mentoring sales talent is a key responsibility of sales leaders. By investing in the professional growth and development of their teams, sales leaders can cultivate future leaders, enhance team capabilities, and drive long-term success.

Benefits:

- **Leadership Development:** Cultivate future leaders and

develop leadership skills within your team.
- **Skill Enhancement:** Improve team capabilities through targeted training and mentoring.
- **Career Growth:** Support the career growth and development of your team members.

10.5 Strategic Vision and Decision-Making

Sales leaders are responsible for setting strategic vision, making informed decisions, and steering their teams towards success. By analysing market trends, identifying opportunities, and making data-driven decisions, sales leaders can position their teams for success and achieve their sales objectives.

Benefits:

- **Strategic Alignment:** Align team efforts with organisational goals and objectives.
- **Opportunity Identification:** Identify and capitalise on new opportunities for growth.
- **Informed Decisions:** Make informed, data-driven decisions to drive success.

Mastering sales leadership is essential for driving team success, fostering a culture of excellence, and achieving organisational goals. By leading by example, communicating effectively, collaborating with your team, developing and mentoring sales talent, and making strategic decisions, you can become an effective and influential sales leader who inspires and guides their team to success.

In the following chapters, we'll delve deeper into specific leadership strategies, techniques, and best practices to help you master sales leadership and achieve dynamic sales mastery.

BUILDING A PERSONAL BRAND

11.1 Understanding Personal Branding

Personal branding in sales is about distinguishing yourself from competitors and creating a unique value proposition for your clients. It involves communicating your strengths, skills, and values in a consistent manner that resonates with your target audience.

Benefits:

- **Differentiation:** Stand out in a crowded market by highlighting what makes you unique.
- **Trust Building:** Foster trust and credibility with potential clients by showcasing your expertise and consistency.
- **Career Advancement:** Enhance your career opportunities through a strong, recognisable personal brand.

11.2 Crafting Your Brand Message

Your brand message is the core of your personal branding strategy. It should clearly articulate who you are, what you stand for, and the unique benefits you offer. This message must be compelling, memorable, and reflective of your professional identity.

Benefits:

- **Clarity:** Provide clear, concise information about your value to customers.
- **Engagement:** Engage your audience with a compelling narrative that captures their interest.
- **Consistency:** Maintain consistency in your message across all platforms to reinforce your brand identity.

11.3 Visibility and Presence

Building visibility and maintaining a presence both online and offline are critical for personal branding. This includes active engagement on social media, networking events, speaking engagements, and publishing relevant content in your field.

Benefits:

- **Reach:** Extend your reach and influence by being visible where your clients are.
- **Engagement:** Increase engagement with your audience by being actively involved in discussions and events.
- **Influence:** Establish yourself as a thought leader in your industry.

11.4 Leveraging Social Media

Social media platforms are powerful tools for building and promoting your personal brand. They provide opportunities to share insights, join conversations, and connect with peers and potential clients, thus amplifying your professional presence.

Benefits:

- **Connectivity:** Connect with a broader audience across geographical boundaries.

- **Real-Time Feedback:** Gain real-time feedback on your ideas and content, helping you refine your approach.
- **Brand Amplification:** Use social media to amplify your brand and reach more potential clients.

11.5 Networking and Relationships

Networking is vital for personal branding. Building strong relationships within your industry can lead to new opportunities, partnerships, and a robust referral network. Effective networking involves genuine engagement and mutual value exchange.

Benefits:

- **Opportunity Generation:** Create new business opportunities through effective networking.
- **Partnerships:** Forge partnerships that can elevate your brand and extend your market reach.
- **Referrals:** Benefit from a strong referral network that boosts your credibility and sales potential.

11.6 Continual Learning and Adaptation

The final aspect of building a personal brand is the commitment to continual learning and adaptation. The market evolves, and so should your brand. Staying updated with industry trends and continuously refining your skills are crucial for maintaining relevance and effectiveness.

Benefits:

- **Relevance:** Stay relevant in the ever-changing market environment.
- **Skill Enhancement:** Continuously enhance your skills to meet the growing demands of your industry.
- **Innovation:** Foster innovation in your approach to

personal branding and sales strategies.

Building a personal brand is a strategic approach to establishing your identity as a sales professional. It encompasses understanding and crafting your brand message, enhancing visibility, leveraging digital platforms, networking effectively, and committing to ongoing learning and adaptation.

ACHIEVING WORK-LIFE BALANCE

12.1 Understanding Work-Life Balance

Work-life balance involves managing professional responsibilities and personal life in a way that reduces stress and prevents burnout. For sales professionals, achieving this balance is crucial for maintaining long-term productivity and personal well-being.

Benefits:

- **Reduced Stress:** Minimise work-related stress by maintaining a healthy balance.
- **Increased Productivity:** Improve overall productivity by being well-rested and mentally clear.
- **Enhanced Well-being:** Enhance personal well-being by ensuring time for rest and personal activities.

12.2 Setting Boundaries

Setting clear boundaries is essential for achieving work-life balance. It involves defining and communicating your work limits and expectations to colleagues and clients, ensuring that personal time remains protected.

Benefits:

- **Control Over Time:** Gain more control over your personal and professional time.
- **Respect for Personal Time:** Encourage respect from others towards your non-working hours.
- **Reduced Burnout:** Prevent burnout by clearly delineating work time from personal time.

12.3 Time Management Skills

Effective time management is crucial for achieving a work-life balance. Sales professionals must prioritise tasks, set realistic goals, and use tools to efficiently manage time to ensure they can fulfil work obligations while also dedicating time to personal life.

Benefits:

- **Efficiency:** Increase efficiency by prioritising tasks and managing time well.
- **Goal Achievement:** Achieve professional and personal goals through effective planning.
- **Personal Fulfilment:** Attain personal fulfilment by allocating time for personal interests and family.

12.4 The Role of Technology

Leveraging technology can significantly aid in achieving work-life balance. From calendar apps to productivity tools, technology can help streamline tasks, set reminders, and even block time for breaks and personal activities.

Benefits:

- **Streamlined Processes:** Use technology to streamline work processes and save time.
- **Scheduled Downtime:** Employ apps to schedule downtime effectively.

- **Enhanced Organisation:** Stay organised and on track with both work and personal activities.

12.5 Building Support Systems

A strong support system at work and at home can facilitate better work-life balance. This includes supportive coworkers, understanding leadership, and family members who appreciate the demands of a sales career.

Benefits:

- **Emotional Support:** Receive emotional support from both personal and professional contacts.
- **Shared Responsibilities:** Share responsibilities at work and home to reduce personal burden.
- **Increased Stability:** Experience increased stability and less stress with a supportive network.

12.6 Regular Self-Assessment

Regular self-assessment is necessary to maintain work-life balance. Evaluating your current balance on a regular basis can help identify areas of improvement, adjust strategies, and make changes to better meet your personal and professional needs.

Benefits:

- **Continuous Improvement:** Continually improve strategies for balancing work and life.
- **Adaptability:** Adapt to life changes effectively by reassessing balance needs.
- **Personal Growth:** Foster personal growth by reflecting on and adjusting life priorities.

Achieving work-life balance is a continuous process that requires commitment, strategy, and the ability to adjust as circumstances change. For sales professionals, mastering this balance is essential not only for career longevity but also for maintaining a fulfilling personal life.

ACKNOWLEDGMENTS

To our readers,

Thank you for embarking on this journey through "Dynamic Sales Mastery: Empowering Sales Professionals." We are deeply grateful for your trust in choosing this book as your guide to mastering the art and science of sales.

Sales is an ever-evolving field, filled with challenges and opportunities alike. The mastery of dynamic sales skills not only enhances your professional capabilities but also opens doors to unparalleled success and personal growth.

Benefits of Dynamic Sales Mastery for You

- **Career Advancement:** Elevate your career by mastering proven sales techniques and strategies.
- **Increased Revenue:** Boost your sales performance and contribute to your organisation's growth.
- **Personal Growth:** Develop essential soft skills like communication, negotiation, and leadership that benefit you both professionally and personally.
- **Job Satisfaction:** Achieve greater satisfaction and fulfilment in your sales role by continuously improving and achieving your goals.
- **Work-Life Balance:** Learn to manage your time effectively, reduce stress, and achieve a better work-life balance, enhancing your overall well-being.

We would like to extend our heartfelt gratitude to our dedicated team who contributed to the creation of this book. Your hard work, expertise, and commitment to excellence have been invaluable.

We also wish to thank our mentors, colleagues, and industry experts whose insights and wisdom have enriched this book. Your guidance has been instrumental in shaping its content and ensuring its relevance to today's sales landscape.

Last but not least, a special thank you to our readers for your continued support and engagement. Your feedback and success stories inspire us to keep striving for excellence and providing you with valuable content that empowers you in your sales journey.

Remember, mastery is a journey, not a destination. We encourage you to apply the principles and strategies outlined in this book, adapt them to your unique circumstances, and continue your pursuit of dynamic sales mastery.

You can join our Facebook community here www.facebook.com/groups/dynamicsalesmastery/

Wishing you all the best in your sales endeavours and personal growth journey.

Warm regards,

Sanjay Nakrani

www.ingramcontent.com/pod-product-compliance
Lightning Source LLC
Chambersburg PA
CBHW070420230526
45471CB00006B/2899